J74.5 chantler

W9-AFT-765

THE SIGN of the BLACK ROCK

THREE THIEVES · BOOK TWO

DELPHI PUBLIC LIBRARY

222 East Main Street
Delphi, Indiana 46923
765-564-2929

Text and illustrations © 2011 Scott Chantler

All rights reserved. No part of this publication may be reproduced, stored in a retrieval system or transmitted, in any form or by any means, without the prior written permission of Kids Can Press Ltd. or, in case of photocopying or other reprographic copying, a license from The Canadian Copyright Licensing Agency (Access Copyright). For an Access Copyright license, visit www.accesscopyright.ca or call toll free to 1-800-893-5777.

This is a work of fiction and any resemblance of characters to persons living or dead is purely coincidental.

Kids Can Press acknowledges the financial support of the Government of Ontario, through the Ontario Media Development Corporation's Ontario Book Initiative; the Ontario Arts Council; the Canada Council for the Arts; and the Government of Canada, through the BPIDP, for our publishing activity.

Published in Canada by
Kids Can Press Ltd.
25 Dockside Drive
Toronto, ON M5A 0B5

Published in the U.S. by
Kids Can Press Ltd.
2250 Military Road
Tonawanda, NY 14150

www.kidscanpress.com

Edited by Karen Li
Designed by Rachel Di Salle and Scott Chantler
Pages lettered with Blambot comic fonts

The hardcover edition of this book is smyth sewn casebound.
The paperback edition of this book is limp sewn with a drawn-on cover.
Manufactured in Buji, Shenzhen, China, in 4/2011 by WKT Company

CM 11 0 9 8 7 6 5 4 3 2 1
CM PA 11 0 9 8 7 6 5 4 3 2 1

Library and Archives Canada Cataloguing in Publication

Chantler, Scott
     The sign of the black rock / Scott Chantler.

(Three thieves ; bk. 2)
ISBN 978-1-55453-416-6 (bound). —ISBN 978-1-55453-417-3 (pbk.)

I. Title. II. Series: Chantler, Scott. Three thieves ; bk. 2.

PN6733.C53S54 2011   j741.5   C2011-900091-1

Kids Can Press is a /ᐤrus™ Entertainment company

THE SIGN of the BLACK ROCK

THREE THIEVES · BOOK TWO

Scott Chantler

Kids Can Press

ACT ONE

STORM

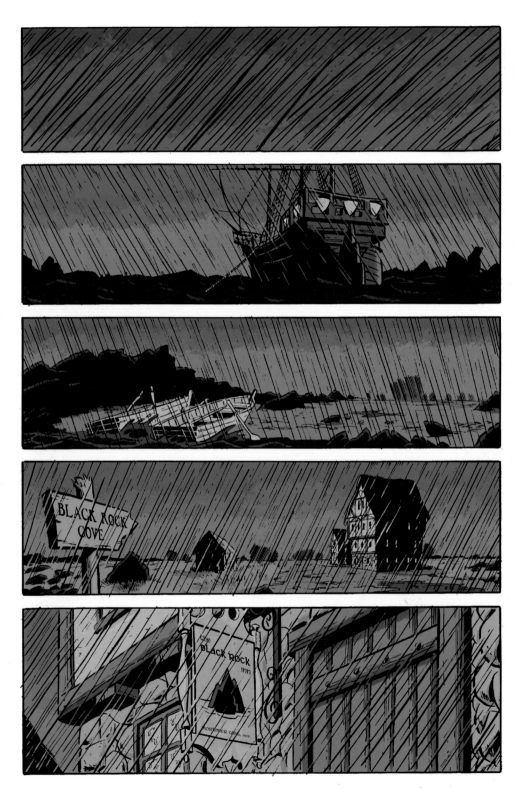

9

11

14

16

17

BESIDES, IT SEEMS RATHER CROWDED IN TH—

?

WELL, HOW DO YOU LIKE *THAT!*

QUIET, TOPPER! I THINK SHE'S TRYING TO TELL US—

DO YOU MEAN THAT WE CAN STAY IN YOUR STABLE? THAT WE CAN SLEEP IN *HERE* TONIGHT?

OH, THANK YOU SO MUCH...THANK YOU THANK YOU *THANK YOU.*

YOU DON'T KNOW WHAT THIS MEANS TO US.

HONESTLY, WE WERE GONNA HAVE TO TIE A *ROPE* AROUND THIS ONE!

WELL, WELL.

CAPTAIN DRAKE, I PRESUME. THIS IS TRULY A RED-LETTER DAY FOR THE BLACK ROCK INN!

YOU'RE CONSIDERED A HERO IN THESE PARTS, CAPTAIN, ON ACCOUNT OF WHAT YOU DID IN THE WAR AGAINST THE LOTHARS.

IF YOU'LL PERMIT ME, I'D LIKE TO BUY YOU A WARM DRINK TO HELP DRY THOSE BONES.

NOW, IF YOU DON'T MIND ME ASKIN', JUST WHAT WOULD BRING THE CAPTAIN OF HER MAJESTY'S OWN DRAGONS HERE TO THE ARMPIT OF NORTH HUNTINGTON ON A NIGHT LIKE THIS?

THE DRAGONS ARE IN PURSUIT OF SOME ESCAPED PRISONERS.

AN ETTIN, A NORKER AND YOUNG GIRL, CORRECT?

YOU'VE HEARD.

WITH THE NUMBER OF CHATTERING WAGTAILS WHO COME THROUGH HERE EVERY DAY, THERE'S NOT MUCH I *DON'T* HEAR.

ANY CHANCE YOU'VE SEEN THEM?

FOLLOW ME!

DON'T WORRY, DESSA... YOU CAN DO IT!

COME ON!

DESSA!

YOU STILL WITH US?

Snap!

Y-YEAH. I'M JUST...

I'M JUST READING THROUGH THIS BOOK OF GREYFALCON'S.

PAH!

I DON'T KNOW WHY YOU'RE STILL LUGGIN' THAT THING AROUND. HAVE YOU ACTUALLY LEARNED ANYTHING FROM IT YET?

YEAH, DESSA. IS THERE ANYTHIN' ABOUT YOUR BROTHER IN THERE, OR WHAT?

NO...

26

28

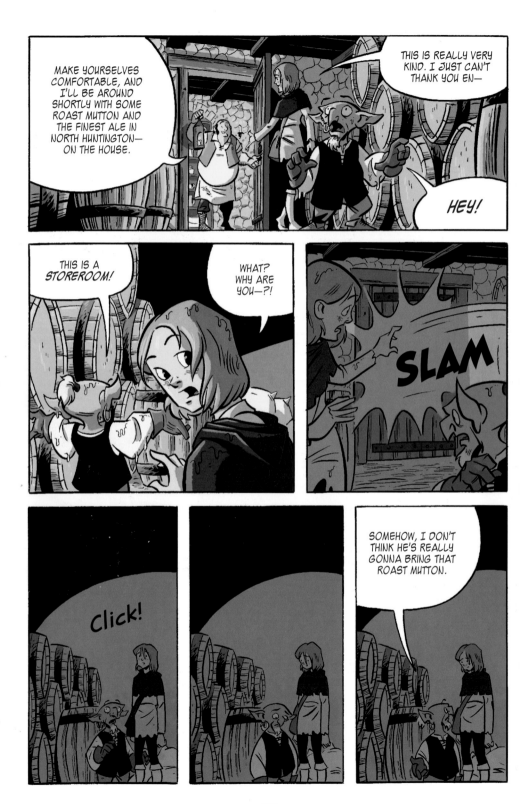

ACT TWO

DISAPPEARING ACT

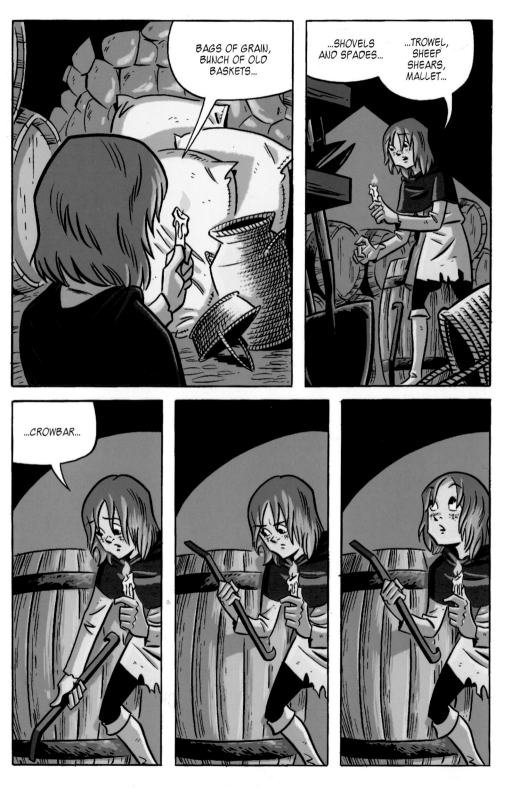

35

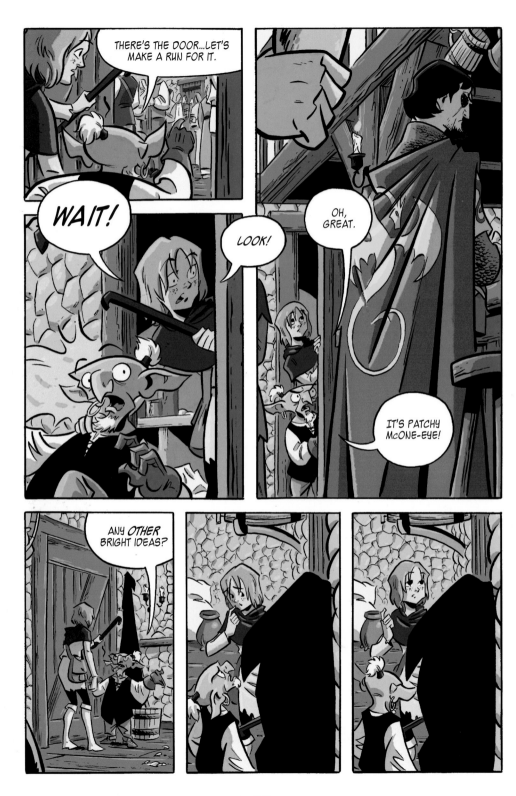

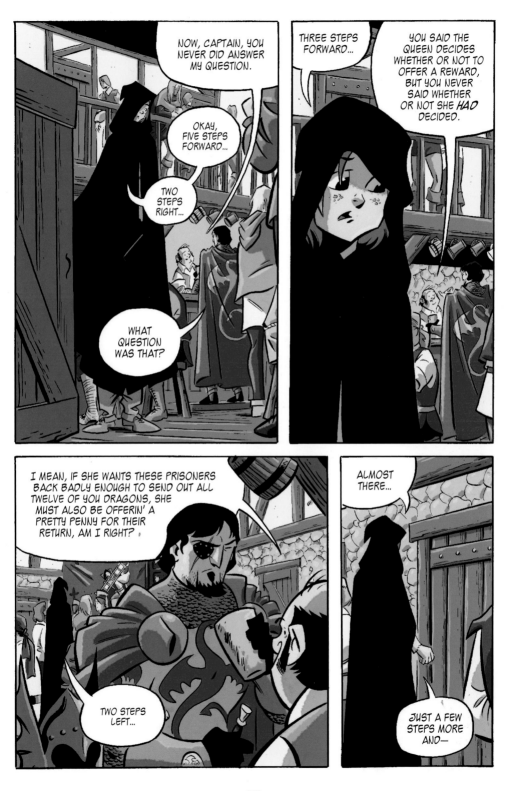

AHH!

RIGHT! HARD RIGHT!

EXCUSE ME, FOLKS! JUST A BIT CLUMSY...! PARDON ME...!

...WHAT I'M SAYIN' IS, IF I KNEW ONE WAY OR THE OTHER, I COULD KEEP MY CUSTOMERS INFORMED AND...

!

WELL, I'LL BE! TWO MORE GENUINE KNIGHTS OF THE REALM, RIGHT HERE IN MY LOWLY ALEHOUSE!

MAY THE HEAVENS BLESS MY ABUNDANT GOOD FORTUNE.

40

41

43

44

45

47

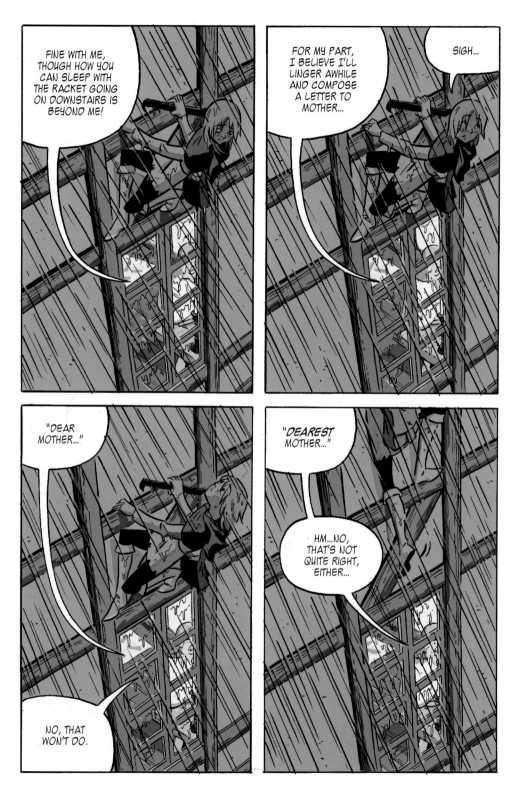

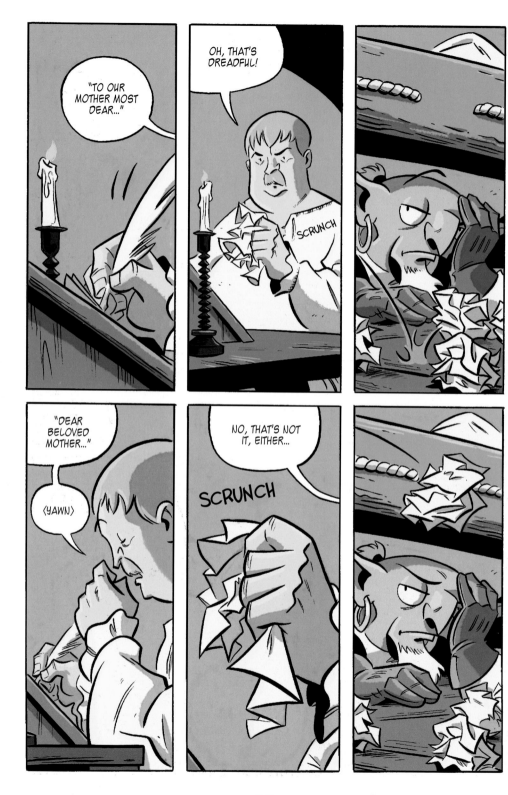

56

60

GRIG, YOU'VE GOT TO GET RID OF THESE QUEEN'S DRAGONS!

TELL ME SOMETHIN' I *DON'T* KNOW, QUINN.

IF THEY MAKE YOU SO BLEEDIN' NERVOUS, WHY DON'T *YOU* LEAVE?

WE CAN'T GO TOO FAR WIT'OUT THE *CREW*, NOW CAN WE? AN' 'OW WOULD IT LOOK, IF 'ALF THE CROWD JUST UP AND LEFT IN THE MIDDLE OF A THUNDERSTORM?

THERE'S THAT...

...AND ALSO THE FACT THAT YOU HAVEN'T *PAID* US YET.

AS USUAL, GETTING MONEY OUT OF YOU HAS BEEN LIKE TRYING TO GET A RIVER TO RUN UPHILL!

THE JINGLIN' OF COINS—THE MORE OF 'EM, THE BETTER—IS A SOUND *ALL THREE* OF US FANCY, UNLESS I'VE SORELY MISJUDGED YOU BOTH.

BUT I'VE NO INTENTION OF PULLIN' OUT THE COFFERS AND HANDIN' A MITT FULL OF GOLD TO A KNOWN SMUGGLER RIGHT UNDER THE NOSE OF ALL TWELVE OF HER MAJESTY'S DRAGONS!

KEEP YER DRESSES ON, LADIES...I'VE GOT AN IDEA HOW TO MAKE 'EM HIT THE ROAD. WHEN THEY DO, YOU'LL GET YER MONEY!

61

63

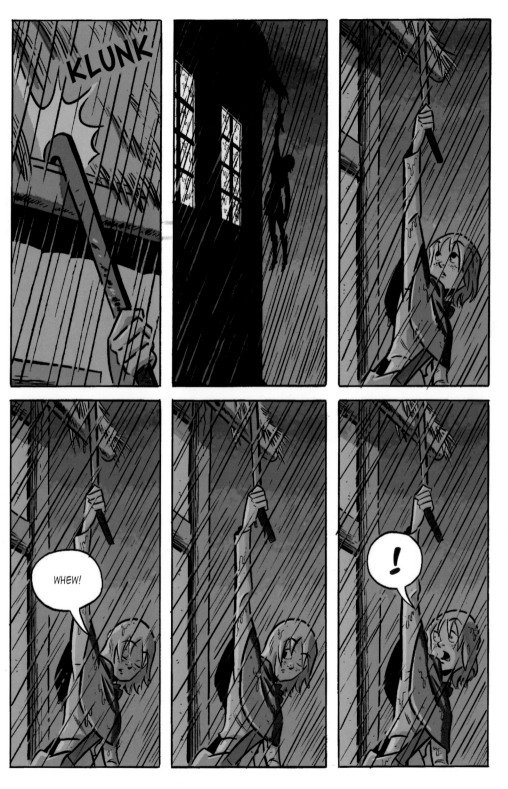

71

73

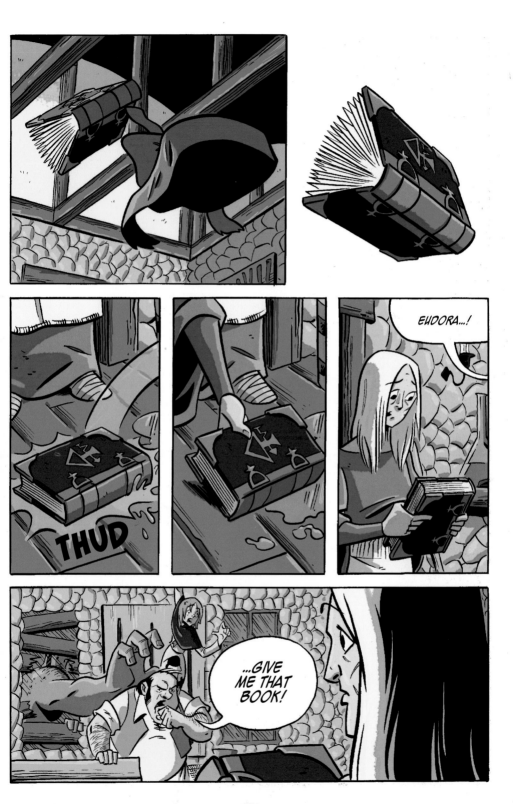

ACT THREE
SCARS

81

82

83

WHAT SEEMS TO BE THE PROBLEM HERE, MEN?

90

91

93

EXCUSE ME?

THE ONLY TWO PEOPLE WHO ACTUALLY SAW THOSE THIEVES AT ALL ARE ME AN' HER...

...AN' *SHE* HASN'T SPOKEN A WORD IN NEARLY TEN YEARS!

YA GOT NO WITNESSES, CAPTAIN. NO EVIDENCE WHATSOEVER THAT THOSE THREE WERE EVER HERE AT ALL.

AN' THE TWO YOU GOT TIED UPSTAIRS WILL BE HAPPY TO TELL ANYONE WHO'LL LISTEN THAT I WAS JUST LYIN' ABOUT IT TO SAVE MY OWN NECK!

NOW YOU AN' ALL THE OTHERS, JUST PACK YOUR THINGS, GET ON YER HORSES...

...AN' *GET OUTTA MY PLACE.*

98

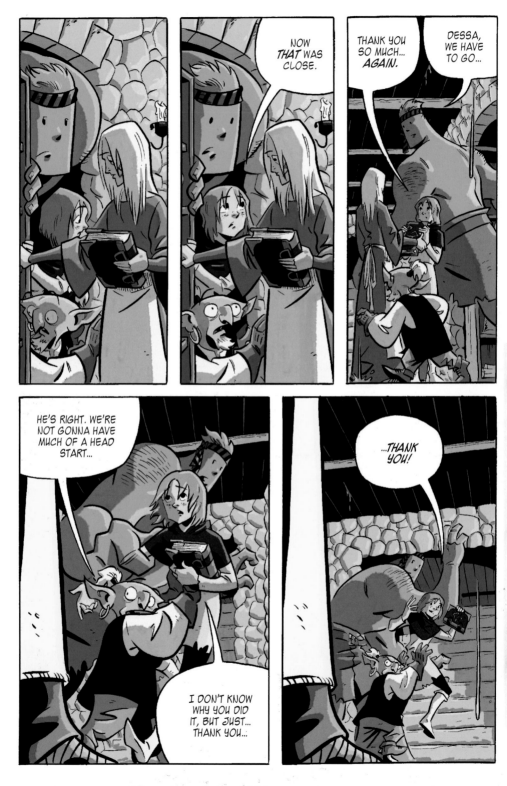

"MY HUSBAND WAS PAID EXTRA FOR THE DISTURBANCE, WHICH OF COURSE WAS ALL HE REALLY CARED ABOUT.

"THEN THE MAN LEFT WITH THE BOY, AND MY HUSBAND ACTED AS IF NOTHING HAD HAPPENED.

"OTHER THAN TO OCCASIONALLY REMIND ME HOW UGLY I LOOKED, OF COURSE.

"HE EVEN APOLOGIZED TO THE MAN FOR THE 'TROUBLE' I'D CAUSED.

"I'D KEPT MY TONGUE, BUT I'D STOPPED USING IT ANYWAY.

WHY DID YOU **STAY** WITH HIM?

HIM, AND THIS PLACE.

"THE WHOLE EPISODE HAD MADE ME NEVER WANT TO SPEAK AGAIN."

I THOUGHT HE LOVED ME, IN HIS WAY. AND HE WAS ALL I HAD.

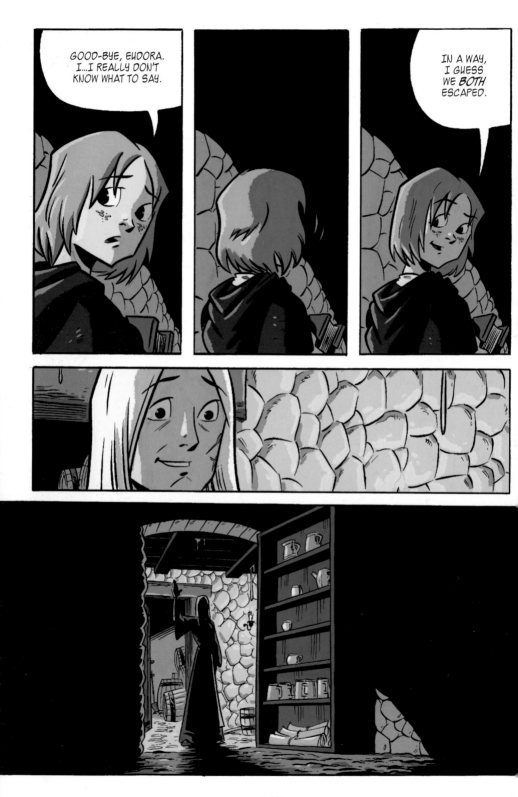

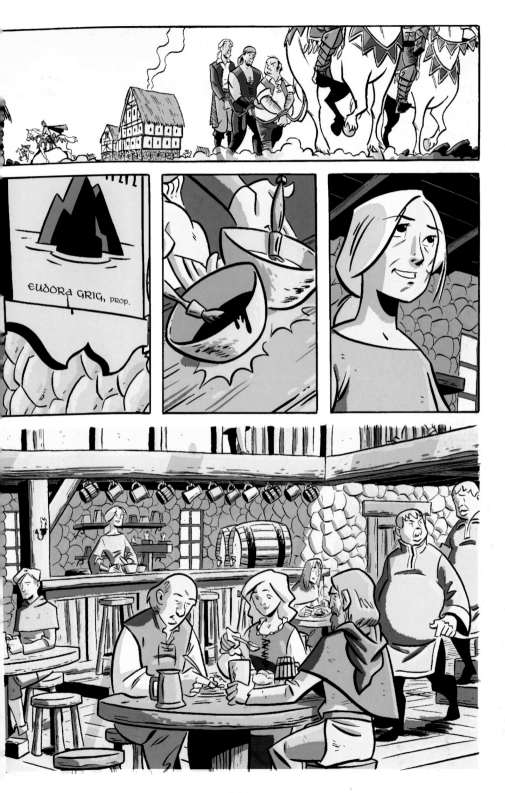